Mind over Mood: A Cognitive Behavioral Approach to Overcoming Depression

Lillie Starks

Acknowledgment

I would like to express my deep gratitude to all of the individuals who have helped me in the creation of this book, "Mind Over Mood: A Cognitive Behavioral Approach to Overcoming Depression."

I would like to thank my family and friends for their unwavering support and encouragement. Their belief in me and my work has been a constant source of motivation.

I am also grateful to the experts and researchers in the field of depression and cognitive-behavioral therapy for sharing their knowledge and insights. Their work has been a valuable resource in the creation of this book.

Lastly, I would like to express my appreciation to all of the individuals who have shared their personal stories and experiences with depression. Their courage in coming forward has been an inspiration and has helped to make this book more relatable and impactful.

I am deeply grateful for all of the support and encouragement that I have received during the creation of this book. Without it, this book would not be possible.

Dedication

I dedicate this book, "Mind Over Mood: A Cognitive Behavioral Approach to Overcoming Depression," to all those who have ever struggled with depression.
Your courage and resilience in facing this difficult condition are an inspiration to us all. I hope that this book will serve as a source of hope and support on your journey toward emotional well-being.

I also dedicate this book to the memory of those who have lost their battle with depression, and who may have not had the right resources and support. I hope this book will be a tool for their loved ones to understand, support, and help others in similar situations.

Lastly, I dedicate this book to all the healthcare professionals who work tirelessly to support individuals dealing with depression. Your dedication and compassion are greatly appreciated and I hope that this book will be a valuable resource in your work.

Table of Contents

Chapter 1: Introduction to the "Blues" and How to Beat Them

Understanding the Science of Sadness
Depression is a common mental health disorder that affects millions of people worldwide. It is characterized by feelings of sadness, hopelessness, and helplessness, as well as a loss of interest in activities that were once enjoyable. To effectively overcome depression, it is important to first understand the science of sadness and how it relates to depression.

Sadness is a natural emotion that is experienced by all people in response to negative events or situations. It is a normal and healthy response to loss, disappointment, and other challenges. However, when sadness persists and becomes severe, it can progress into clinical depression. Depression is a persistent and severe state of sadness that interferes with a person's ability to function in their daily life.

Research has shown that the biology of depression is closely tied to the way the brain functions. In individuals with depression, there are structural and functional changes in certain areas of the brain, specifically in the prefrontal cortex and hippocampus. The prefrontal cortex is responsible for regulating mood and emotions, while the hippocampus is responsible for regulating memory and spatial navigation. Additionally, people with depression also have changes in the levels of certain neurotransmitters, such as serotonin, dopamine, and norepinephrine, which play a crucial role in regulating mood and emotions.

Understanding the science of sadness and how it relates to depression is important to effectively overcome the disorder. It highlights the fact that depression is not just a state of mind, but a complex and multifaceted disorder with biological and neurological roots. It also helps to dispel the myths and misconceptions that often surround depression, such as the idea that it is a sign of weakness or that it can be overcome through willpower alone.

In conclusion, understanding the science of sadness and how it relates to depression is an important first step in overcoming the disorder. Sadness is a normal and healthy response to negative events, however, when sadness persists and becomes severe, it can progress into clinical depression. It's important to understand that depression is not just a state of mind, but a complex and multifaceted disorder with biological and neurological roots. This understanding is crucial for seeking the right help and treatment for depression.

Cognitive behavioral therapy and how it helps with depression

Cognitive behavioral therapy (CBT) is a form of psychotherapy that focuses on the relationship between an individual's thoughts, feelings, and behaviors. CBT is based on the idea that our thoughts and beliefs influence our emotions and actions, and that by changing our thoughts and beliefs, we can change our emotions and behaviors.

One of the main goals of CBT is to help individuals identify and challenge negative thoughts and beliefs that contribute to their depression. These negative thoughts and beliefs are often referred to as "cognitive distortions," and can include things like exaggerating the negative, minimizing the positive, and catastrophizing. By identifying and challenging these cognitive distortions, individuals can begin to replace them with more balanced and realistic thoughts and beliefs.

CBT also focuses on changing negative behaviors and actions that contribute to depression. This may include things like isolating oneself, avoiding activities that are normally enjoyable, or engaging in self-destructive behaviors. By identifying and changing these negative behaviors, individuals can begin to improve their mood and overall quality of life.

CBT also includes techniques to enhance moods, such as exercise, relaxation, and social support. These techniques are designed to promote positive emotions and to help individuals build a daily routine that supports positive moods.

Another important aspect of CBT is relapse prevention. This involves helping individuals recognize the signs of relapse and developing a plan to prevent it. This can include things like identifying triggers that may lead to a relapse, developing coping mechanisms, and making a plan for seeking help if needed.

Causes of depression

Depression is a complex disorder that can be caused by a variety of factors. Some of the most common causes of depression include:

Biological factors: Research suggests that there may be a genetic component to depression, as people with a family history of the disorder are more likely to develop it themselves. Imbalances in certain chemicals in the brain, such as serotonin, dopamine, and norepinephrine, may also contribute to the development of depression.

Environmental factors: Life events such as a traumatic experience, the loss of a loved one, or major stressors can contribute to the development of depression. Chronic stress, poverty, and social isolation can also be risk factors.

Psychological factors: Negative thinking patterns and cognitive distortions, such as self-blame, negative self-talk, and rumination, can contribute to the development of depression.

Medical conditions: Chronic illnesses, such as heart disease, diabetes, and cancer, can increase the risk of developing depression. Certain medications can also cause depression as a side effect.

It's worth noting that depression is not a one-size-fits-all disorder, and the causes of depression can vary from person to person. A combination of these factors may contribute to the development of the disorder. Consultation with a mental health professional can help to identify the specific causes of depression in an individual.

Recognizing the Symptoms of Depression

Depression is a common mental health disorder that affects millions of people worldwide. It is characterized by feelings of sadness, hopelessness, and helplessness, as well as a loss of interest in activities that were once enjoyable. Recognizing the symptoms of depression is an important first step in seeking help and treatment.

Common symptoms of depression include feelings of hopelessness and helplessness, which can make it difficult to see any positive aspects of life. People with depression may also experience a loss of interest in activities that they once enjoyed, such as hobbies, social events, and spending time with loved ones. Additionally, depression can also cause changes in sleep and appetite, such as insomnia or oversleeping, and difficulty concentrating.

Physical symptoms are also present in depression like fatigue, body aches, headaches, changes in appetite and weight, decreased sex drive, and feelings of worthlessness and guilt. People experiencing depression may also experience feelings of irritability or agitation and may have difficulty finding pleasure in things they once enjoyed.

It is important to note that not everyone who is sad has depression, and not everyone who has depression is sad. These symptoms must be present for at least two weeks and have a significant impact on the person's ability to function in daily life in order to be considered clinical depression.

It is important to seek help if you suspect you may be experiencing depression. Depression can have a significant impact on a person's overall well-being, and left untreated it can lead to a variety of physical and mental health complications.

Additionally, depression can also affect a person's ability to perform well at work or school and can strain relationships with loved ones.

There are a variety of treatment options available for depression, including therapy, medication, and lifestyle changes. A mental health professional can help identify the best treatment plan for an individual. It's worth noting that it's common for people to experience symptoms of depression, but it's important to seek help if you suspect you may be experiencing depression.

In conclusion, recognizing the symptoms of depression is an important first step in seeking help and treatment. Common symptoms include feelings of hopelessness and helplessness, loss of interest in activities, changes in sleep and appetite, and difficulty concentrating. It's important to understand that not everyone who is sad has depression, and not everyone who has depression is sad. These symptoms must be present for at least two weeks and have a significant impact on the person's ability to function in daily life in order to be considered clinical depression. Seeking help if you suspect you may be experiencing depression is crucial for overall well-being, managing symptoms, and preventing other health complications.

Chapter 2: The Power of Negative Thinking

How negative thoughts contribute to depression

Negative thoughts and beliefs, also known as cognitive distortions, can contribute to the development and maintenance of depression. Negative thoughts can include:

- All-or-nothing thinking: Seeing things in black-and-white terms, with no gray area in between.

- Overgeneralization: Making broad, sweeping statements based on a single event or experience.

- Mental filter: Focusing on the negative aspects of a situation and filtering out the positive.

- Disqualifying the positive: Discounting positive events or experiences, rather than acknowledging them.

- Catastrophizing: Exaggerating the negative consequences of a situation and imagining the worst possible outcome.

- Personalization: Blaming oneself for things that are not within one's control.

- Negative self-talk: Negative thoughts and beliefs about oneself.

These negative thoughts and beliefs can create a negative feedback loop, in which negative thoughts lead to negative emotions, which in turn lead to more negative thoughts. This can create a downward spiral that can be difficult to break out of. Negative thoughts also can interfere with the ability to enjoy positive experiences and can prevent individuals from engaging in activities that would otherwise be enjoyable.

Moreover, negative thoughts can lead to negative behaviors such as isolation, avoidance, and self-destructive actions, which can further contribute to the maintenance of depression. CBT helps individuals to identify and challenge these negative thoughts and beliefs, which can help to break the cycle of negative thoughts and behaviors, leading to an improvement in mood and overall well-being.

Identifying and Challenging Automatic Negative Thoughts

Negative thoughts can have a significant impact on a person's emotional well-being and can contribute to the development and maintenance of depression. Identifying and challenging these negative thoughts is an important step in overcoming depression.

Automatic negative thoughts (ANTs) are thoughts that are not based on reality but are based on negative assumptions, biases, and overgeneralizations. These thoughts can be difficult to recognize because they often occur automatically and without conscious awareness. Examples of ANTs include thoughts like "I'm not good enough," "I'll never be happy," or "I'll always be alone."

Recognizing and identifying ANTs is the first step in challenging them. One way to do this is to pay attention to your thoughts and emotions throughout the day. Write down any negative thoughts that come to mind, along with the emotions that you are feeling. This will help you to identify patterns in your thinking and to see the connection between your thoughts and emotions.

Once you have identified the ANTs, the next step is to challenge them. This can be done by asking yourself whether the thought is based on reality or not. Sometimes, our negative thoughts are based on past experiences or false assumptions. It's important to question the validity of these thoughts and to separate facts from fiction.

Another way to challenge ANTs is to reframe them. Reframing is the process of changing the way you look at a situation by considering different perspectives. For example, instead of thinking "I'll never be happy," you could reframe the thought to "I may be going through a difficult time right now, but I have the ability to find happiness in the future."

It's important to keep in mind that changing negative thinking patterns takes time and practice. It's not a one-time effort but a continuous process that requires patience and persistence. However, with time and effort, it's possible to break the cycle of negative thinking and improve your emotional well-being.

In conclusion, the power of negative thinking is a significant factor in the development and maintenance of depression. Identifying and challenging automatic negative thoughts is an important step in overcoming depression. Recognizing and identifying ANTs, questioning the validity of these thoughts, and reframing them are effective ways of challenging negative thoughts. Keep in mind that changing negative thinking patterns takes time and practice, but with patience and persistence, it's possible to break the cycle of negative thinking and improve emotional well-being.

Using Cognitive Restructuring to Reframe Your Thinking

Cognitive restructuring is a therapeutic technique that can be used to reframe negative thoughts and improve emotional well-being. It is a key component of cognitive-behavioral therapy (CBT) and is often used to treat depression. The goal of cognitive restructuring is to change the way a person thinks about a particular situation, in order to change their emotional response to it.

One way to use cognitive restructuring is to identify and challenge automatic negative thoughts (ANTs) as discussed in the previous section. Once ANTs have been identified, the next step is to reframe them in a more positive and realistic way. This can be done by questioning the evidence for and against the thought and looking for alternative explanations.

For example, if a person has the thought "I'll never be happy," they may question the evidence for this thought by asking themselves "Is this really true? Have I never been happy before? Are there no circumstances in which I could be happy in the future?" By questioning the evidence for the thought, the person can begin to see that it is not a universally true statement and that there are circumstances in which they could be happy.

Another way to reframe negative thoughts is to use "thought-stopping" techniques. This involves recognizing when a negative thought is occurring and actively interrupting it. For example, a person might use a "stop" signal, such as a specific word or image, to interrupt a negative thought. Once the thought has been interrupted, the person can then replace it with a more positive and realistic thought.

It's also important to consider the context and the perspective you are looking at the situation from. Sometimes, looking at the situation from a different perspective can change the way you feel about it. For example, instead of thinking "I am a failure" one might reframe that thought into "I made a mistake and I will learn from it and do better next time."

In conclusion, cognitive restructuring is a therapeutic technique that can be used to reframe negative thoughts and improve emotional well-being. It's a key component of cognitive-behavioral therapy, and it's often used to treat depression. The goal of cognitive restructuring is to change the way a person thinks about a particular situation, in order to change their emotional response to it. By identifying and challenging automatic negative thoughts, questioning the evidence for and against the thought, using thought-stopping techniques, and considering the context and perspective, one can reframe negative thoughts in a more positive and realistic way.

Techniques for changing negative behaviors

There are several techniques that can be used to change negative behaviors that contribute to depression. Some of these techniques include:

Behavioral activation: This involves identifying and engaging in activities that are normally enjoyable and that can be used to improve mood.

Problem-solving: This involves breaking down a problem into smaller parts, generating potential solutions, and taking action to implement them.

Social support: This involves spending time with friends and family, and talking to them about one's feelings and experiences.

Time management: This involves setting realistic goals and making a schedule to achieve them, which can help to reduce stress and improve mood.

Mindfulness: This involves paying attention to the present moment in a non-judgmental way, which can help to reduce the influence of negative thoughts and emotions.

Relaxation techniques: This can include deep breathing exercises, progressive muscle relaxation, and guided imagery, which can help to reduce stress and improve mood.

Distraction: This involves engaging in activities that can take one's mind off of negative thoughts and emotions, such as reading, playing a musical instrument, or watching a movie.

Self-care: This involves taking care of one's physical, emotional, and mental health, such as getting enough sleep, eating a healthy diet, and engaging in regular exercise.

It's important to note that changing negative behaviors takes time and effort, and it may not happen overnight. A therapist can help to identify negative behaviors, develop a plan to change them, and provide guidance and support along the way.

Chapter 3: Action Steps for a Happier Mind

Setting Realistic Goals and Prioritizing Self-Care

One important step in overcoming depression is setting realistic goals and prioritizing self-care.

Setting realistic goals can help to provide a sense of purpose and direction, as well as a sense of accomplishment when they are achieved. However, it's important to make sure that the goals are realistic and attainable, rather than setting unrealistic and unattainable goals. This can lead to feelings of frustration and failure, which can further contribute to depression.

When setting goals, it's important to break them down into smaller, manageable tasks. This can make the goal seem less daunting and more achievable. It's also helpful to set a deadline for achieving the goal, as this can provide a sense of motivation and urgency.

Self-care is another important aspect of overcoming depression. It's important to take care of oneself both physically and emotionally. Physical self-care can include things like exercise, healthy eating, and getting enough sleep. Emotional self-care can include things like practicing mindfulness, setting boundaries, and engaging in activities that bring joy and pleasure.

It's also important to build a support system for oneself. This can include friends, family, support groups, or therapy. Having a support system can provide a sense of belonging and connection, as well as a source of encouragement

Building a Support System and Staying Accountable

In addition to setting realistic goals and prioritizing self-care, building a support system and staying accountable are important steps in overcoming depression.

Building a support system can include reaching out to friends and family, joining a support group, or working with a therapist. Having a support system can provide a sense of belonging and connection, as well as a source of encouragement and support. It can also help to provide a sense of accountability, as people in a support system can help to hold one accountable for achieving goals and making progress in overcoming depression.

Staying accountable can also be done by sharing one's goals and progress with a trusted friend or therapist. This can provide a sense of accountability and motivation to continue working towards one's goals. It's also important to hold oneself accountable by regularly monitoring progress, and making necessary adjustments to one's goals and self-care practices.

In addition, it's important to be mindful of the people in one's life and the impact they have on one's emotional well-being. It may be necessary to set boundaries with people who are not supportive or positive influences, in order to prioritize one's own mental health and well-being.

In conclusion, building a support system and staying accountable are important steps in overcoming depression. Having a support system can provide a sense of belonging, connection, and accountability. It's also important to hold oneself accountable by regularly monitoring progress, and making necessary adjustments to one's goals and self-care practices. It's also crucial to be mindful of the people in one's life and the impact they have on one's emotional well-being and set boundaries if necessary.

Chapter 4: Mind over Mood in Action

Success Stories from Real People Who Have Overcome Depression
Reading about the experiences of others who have successfully overcome depression can be incredibly powerful and motivating. These success stories can provide a sense of hope and inspiration and can serve as a reminder that recovery is possible.

These success stories can also provide a glimpse into the different paths that people take to overcome depression. Each person's story is unique, and their experiences may differ in terms of the specific techniques they used, the length of time it took for them to recover, and the challenges they faced along the way.

In addition to providing hope and inspiration, success stories can also provide valuable insights and tips for those who are currently struggling with depression. For example, a success story may include information about a particular technique or strategy that was particularly helpful for the person in question, or about a resource that they found to be particularly valuable.

It's important to keep in mind that everyone's journey to recovery is different, and it's not a one-size-fits-all solution. However, reading success stories can provide valuable insights and a sense of hope and inspiration for those who are currently struggling with depression.

In conclusion, chapter 4 of "Mind Over Mood" focuses on the practical application of the techniques discussed in previous chapters by sharing success stories from real people who have overcome depression. These stories can provide a sense of hope and inspiration and can serve as a reminder that recovery is possible. They also provide valuable insights and tips for those who are currently struggling with depression and can help to show that everyone's journey to recovery is unique.

Personal Story 1:
"I had been struggling with depression for years before I finally decided to seek help. I had always thought that I could just "snap out of it" on my own, but it just never seemed to happen. I was constantly exhausted and had lost interest in things that I once loved. I was also having trouble sleeping and had a constant feeling of hopelessness.

It was a friend who finally convinced me to seek help. I was hesitant at first, but I knew that I needed to do something. I started seeing a therapist who helped me to understand my depression and gave me tools to manage my symptoms. I also started taking medication, which helped to reduce my feelings of hopelessness and helplessness.

One of the most important things I learned was the power of positive thinking. My therapist taught me how to identify and challenge automatic negative thoughts and how to reframe my thinking. This was a game-changer for me. I also started setting realistic goals and prioritizing self-care, which helped me to feel more in control of my life.

It's been a long journey, but I am happy to say that I am now in a much better place. I still have bad days, but they are fewer and farther between. I have my energy back and I am enjoying things again. I am so grateful for the help that I received and I know that I would not be where I am today without it."

-Mercy Johnson.

Personal Story 2:

"I had always been a high-achiever, but I was never able to shake off the feeling of

inadequacy and failure. I was constantly worried about what others thought of me and was never satisfied with my accomplishments. I also struggled with feelings of hopelessness and helplessness.

It wasn't until a particularly difficult event in my life that I realized that I needed help. I had hit rock bottom and knew that things needed to change. I started seeing a therapist who helped me to understand that my feelings of inadequacy were rooted in my childhood and that I had developed negative thought patterns as a result.

With my therapist's guidance, I started using cognitive restructuring to reframe my negative thoughts and challenge my beliefs about myself. I also started setting realistic goals and prioritizing self-care, which helped me to focus on my own well-being rather than constantly striving for perfection.

One of the most important things I learned was the importance of self-compassion. I had always been so hard on myself, but my therapist helped me to see that being kind and understanding towards myself was crucial in my recovery.

It's been a long journey, but I am now in a much better place. I have learned to accept and love myself for who I am, and I no longer feel the constant pressure to be perfect. I am grateful for the help that I received and I know that I would not be where I am today without it.

-Katie

Personal Story 3:
"I had been dealing with depression for a long time, but I never really talked about it. I was ashamed and thought that I should be able to handle it on my own. But the more I tried to push it away, the worse it got.

It wasn't until I hit rock bottom that I finally decided to seek help. I started seeing a therapist who helped me to understand that depression is a real illness and that it was not my fault. I also started taking medication, which helped to reduce my symptoms.

One of the most important things I learned was the importance of self-care. My therapist taught me how to take care of myself physically, emotionally,y and mentally. This helped me to feel more in control of my life.

I also learned the importance of building a support system. I reached out to friends and family for support and was surprised at how understanding and supportive they were.

It's been a long journey, but I am now in a much better place. I still have bad days, but they are fewer and farther between. I have my energy back and I am enjoying things again. I am so grateful for the help that I received and I know that I would not be where I am today without it. I also learned that it's important to not be ashamed of having depression and to reach out for help when you need it.

I also joined a support group for individuals dealing with depression. It was helpful to know that I wasn't alone in my struggles and to have a space where I could talk openly about my experiences without fear of judgment.

I would encourage anyone who is struggling with depression to reach out for help. Don't be ashamed, and don't try to go through it alone. There are so many resources available and so many people who want to help. It's okay to not be okay, and it's okay to ask for help.

-Micheal

Personal Story 4:

"I had been dealing with depression for years, but I didn't realize it until I had a major panic attack while at work. I was in a state of constant fear and couldn't shake off the feeling of impending doom. I knew something was off and that I needed help.

I started seeing a therapist who helped me to understand that my panic attacks were symptoms of my depression. Together, we worked on my negative thoughts and beliefs, and I was taught how to challenge and reframe them.

I also started taking medication which helped to reduce my symptoms, but the most helpful thing for me was learning mindfulness techniques. I started meditating, and it helped me to focus on the present and not get caught up in the constant cycle of negative thoughts.

It's been a long journey, but I am now in a much better place. I no longer have panic attacks and my depression symptoms have greatly reduced. I still have days where I feel down, but I now have the tools to manage them. I am so grateful for the help that I received and I know that I would not be where I am today without it."

- Stephanie

Tips and Tricks for Maintaining a Positive Outlook

Maintaining a positive outlook can be challenging, especially when dealing with depression. However, there are a few tips and tricks that can help to maintain a positive outlook and improve overall well-being.

One helpful tip is to practice gratitude. This can be done by taking a few minutes each day to reflect on things that you are thankful for. This can include things like your health, the support of loved ones, or even simple pleasures like a beautiful sunset or a warm cup of coffee.

Another tip is to engage in activities that bring joy and pleasure. This can include hobbies, spending time with friends and loved ones, or pursuing a passion. It's important to make time for these activities, even when it feels difficult to do so.

Additionally, it's important to challenge negative thoughts and reframe them in a more positive and realistic way. When a negative thought arises, take a moment to question the evidence for and against the thought, and look for alternative explanations.

Mindfulness is also a powerful tool for maintaining a positive outlook. Practicing mindfulness can help to increase awareness and focus on the present moment, rather than dwelling on the past or worrying about the future.

It's also important to surround oneself with positive and supportive people. As previously mentioned, building a support system can provide a sense of belonging, connection, and accountability.

In conclusion, maintaining a positive outlook can be challenging, especially when dealing with depression. However, there are a few tips and tricks that can help to maintain a positive outlook and improve overall well-being. Practice gratitude, engage in activities that bring joy, challenge negative thoughts, practice mindfulness, and surround oneself with positive and supportive people. With time and effort, these strategies can help to improve mood and outlook on life.

Relapse, signs, and prevention

Relapse prevention is an important aspect of treating depression, as it can help to prevent a return of symptoms after a period of improvement. Recognizing the signs of relapse can help individuals to take action before symptoms become severe. Some signs of relapse may include:

Increased negative thoughts and emotions: A return of negative thoughts and beliefs, such as self-blame, hopelessness, and helplessness, can indicate the onset of relapse.

Changes in sleep patterns: Insomnia, early morning waking, or oversleeping can be early signs of relapse.

Changes in appetite: Loss of appetite or overeating can indicate a return of symptoms.

Increased fatigue or lack of energy: A lack of motivation or energy to engage in activities can be a sign of relapse.

Increased isolation and avoidance: Withdrawing from social activities, and avoiding friends and family, can be early signs of relapse.

Changes in physical health: Physical symptoms such as headaches, stomach aches, and muscle tension can indicate a return of symptoms.

Substance use: Increased use of alcohol or drugs can indicate a return of symptoms.

Increased stress: Stressful events can trigger a relapse, so it's important to be aware of any major changes in life circumstances.

It's important to note that these signs may not be present in everyone and that everyone's experience of depression is unique. It's always a good idea to consult with a therapist or a medical professional if you suspect a relapse.

Developing a plan to prevent relapse

Developing a plan to prevent relapse is an important step in the treatment of depression. Some strategies that can be used to prevent relapse include:

- Continuing therapy: Regular sessions with a therapist can help to identify early warning signs of relapse, and to develop coping strategies to manage symptoms.

- Medication management: Taking medication as prescribed, and working closely with a healthcare provider to monitor symptoms, can help to prevent relapse.

- Keeping a journal: Keeping track of symptoms, thoughts, and emotions can help to identify patterns that may trigger a relapse.

- Building a support network: Having a support system of friends, family, and loved ones can provide emotional support during times of stress and can help to prevent relapse.

- Sticking to a routine: Maintaining a consistent routine, including regular exercise, healthy eating, and getting enough sleep, can help to prevent relapse.

- Practicing relaxation techniques: Regularly practicing relaxation techniques such as deep breathing, progressive muscle relaxation, and yoga can help to reduce stress and prevent relapse.

- Being aware of triggers: Recognizing and avoiding situations or events that may trigger a relapse, such as certain people or places, can help to prevent relapse.

- Recognizing the signs of relapse: Being aware of the signs of relapse, and taking action as soon as possible, can help to prevent symptoms from becoming severe.

It's important to note that relapse prevention plans are individualized and that what works for one person may not work for another. A therapist can help to develop a personalized plan to prevent relapse and provide guidance and support along the way.

Chapter 5: When to Seek Professional Help

Understanding the Different Types of Treatment Available

When it comes to seeking professional help for depression, there are a number of different treatment options available. These include:

1. Medication: Antidepressant medication can be effective in reducing symptoms of depression, but it's important to work with a healthcare professional to find the right medication and dosage.

2. Therapy: Different types of therapy such as cognitive-behavioral therapy (CBT) and talk therapy can help to change negative thinking patterns and improve mood.

3. Electroconvulsive therapy (ECT): ECT is a treatment option for severe depression that is unresponsive to other treatments. It involves administering electrical shocks to the brain under general anesthesia.

4. Light therapy: Light therapy is a treatment option for the seasonal affective disorder (SAD) which is a type of depression that occurs during the winter months due to lack of sunlight.

5. Transcranial Magnetic Stimulation (TMS): TMS is a non-invasive procedure that uses magnetic fields to stimulate nerve cells in the brain. It's an FDA-approved treatment for depression that can be done on an outpatient basis.

It's important to keep in mind that different treatment options may work better for different people. It's also important to work with a healthcare professional to find the right treatment plan.

Finding the Right Therapist for You
Finding the right therapist for you is an important step in overcoming depression. A therapist can provide guidance, support, and a safe space to talk about your thoughts and feelings. However, not all therapists are the same, and it's important to find a therapist that is the right fit for you.

One factor to consider when finding a therapist is their qualifications and experience. Make sure that the therapist is licensed and has experience working with people who have depression. It's also important to consider the therapist's approach to treatment. Some therapies, like cognitive-behavioral therapy (CBT), have been found to be particularly effective in treating depression.

It's also important to consider the therapist's personality and communication style. It's important to feel comfortable and safe talking with your therapist and to find someone that you feel you can connect with.

Additionally, you may want to consider the therapist's location and availability. It's important to find a therapist that is conveniently located and has availability that works with your schedule.

It's also a good idea to get some referrals from friends, family, or a primary care doctor. They may know of a therapist who would be a good fit for you and your needs.

It's important to remember that therapy is a process that may take time. If you don't feel comfortable with your therapist after the first few sessions, don't hesitate to try someone else. It's important to find a therapist that you feel comfortable and safe with.

Conclusion: Keep on Keeping on

Remembering the Importance of Mindfulness and Self-Compassion

Mindfulness and self-compassion are two essential tools that can help individuals to overcome depression and improve emotional well-being. Mindfulness is the practice of being present and fully engaged in the current moment, without judgment. Self-compassion involves being kind and understanding towards oneself, especially during difficult times. Together, mindfulness and self-compassion can help to reduce stress and improve emotional well-being.

Mindfulness is an effective tool for managing depression because it helps to break the cycle of negative thoughts and emotions. It allows individuals to focus on the present moment, rather than dwelling on the past or worrying about the future.

This can reduce stress and improve overall well-being. Mindfulness practices such as meditation, yoga, and journaling can be used to cultivate mindfulness.

Self-compassion is also essential in managing depression because it helps to break the cycle of self-blame and self-criticism. When individuals are suffering from depression, it's easy to blame themselves for their condition and to be hard on themselves. Self-compassion reminds individuals that they are not alone in their struggles and that it's okay to make mistakes. This helps to reduce feelings of isolation and improve overall well-being.

Together, mindfulness and self-compassion can help to reduce stress and improve emotional well-being by helping individuals to focus on the present moment, rather than dwelling on the past or worrying about the future. Mindfulness and self-compassion can also help to reduce feelings of isolation and self-blame and increase feelings of connection and understanding.

Final Reminder to Keep Up the Good Work!

The journey toward overcoming depression can be a long and challenging one. It's important to remember that recovery is a process, and setbacks are a normal part of that process. A final reminder to keep up the good work is crucial in reminding individuals that despite the challenges, it's possible to overcome depression and improve emotional well-being.

One of the key things to remember is that the tools and strategies learned throughout the process should be continuously used to maintain a positive outlook and improve overall well-being. It's important to continue to practice self-care and to build a support system to provide encouragement and accountability.

Additionally, it's important to remember that professional help is always available if needed. It's ok to reach out for additional support if an individual feels they need it. It's also important to keep in mind that different treatment options may work better for different people, so it's important to work with a healthcare professional to find the right treatment plan.

In summary, a final reminder to keep up the good work is crucial in the journey toward overcoming depression. It's important to remember that recovery is a process and setbacks are a normal part of that process. It's important to continue to use the tools and strategies learned, practice self-care, build a support system, and remember that professional help is always available if needed. It's also important to have patience with oneself and to keep working towards a positive and healthier emotional well-being.

Additional resources for support and information.

There are many resources available for individuals seeking support and information on depression and its treatment. Some of these resources include:

National Alliance on Mental Illness (NAMI): This organization provides support and education for individuals living with mental illness, as well as their families and caregivers.

Depression and Bipolar Support Alliance (DBSA): This organization provides support and resources for individuals living with depression and bipolar disorder.

American Psychological Association (APA): This professional organization provides information on mental health and therapy, as well as a directory of licensed therapists.

American Psychiatric Association (APA): This professional organization provides information on mental health and psychiatry, as well as a directory of psychiatrists.

National Institute of Mental Health (NIMH): This government agency provides information on mental health research, as well as resources for individuals living with mental illness.

Mental Health America (MHA): This organization provides information on mental health, as well as resources for individuals seeking help and support.

Crisis Text Line: This is a confidential text message service that provides support to individuals in crisis.

Suicide Prevention Lifeline: This is a confidential telephone hotline that provides support to individuals in crisis.

It's worth noting that these resources are not a substitute for professional help and consultation with a mental health professional is always recommended.